S0-BRN-540

A Grandmother's Love for Her Granddaughter during the Coronavirus

Happy Harper Thursdays

Written by Fern Schumer Chapman

Illustrated by Phoebe Chandler Turner

Copyright © 2020 by Fern Schumer Chapman and Phoebe Chandler Turner

All rights reserved. No part of this publication may be reproduced, distributed, or transmitted in any form or by any means, including photocopying, recording, or other electronic or mechanical methods, without the prior written permission of the publisher, except in the case of brief quotations embodied in critical reviews and certain other noncommercial uses permitted by copyright law.

Published April 1, 2020 by Gussie Rose Press, Lake Bluff, Illinois.

Book design by Lorie DeWorken.

ISBN: 978-0-9964725-6-2 (paperback)
ISBN: 978-0-9964725-5-5 (hardcover)

Publisher's Cataloging-in-Publication Data:
   Chapman, Fern Schumer
   Turner, Phoebe Chandler
   Happy Harper Thursdays by Fern Schumer Chapman, Illustrated by Phoebe Chandler Turner
   1.Coronavirus 2. Grandparents 3. Grandchildren 4. Family separation 5. Social distancing 6. Coronavirus – social aspects 7. Bibliotherapy for children 8. children and
      emotional intelligence

For my granddaughter

And for Harper's other grandparents:

Barbara and James Walsh
Cyn Mycoskie and Steve Chapman
Bruce Wasser

And all the grandparents and grandchildren
who have had to endure family separation

After every storm comes a rainbow.

—Unknown

Ever since you were born, you and I have had Happy Harper Thursdays.

We spend the fifth day of the week together. Every single week.

You dig in my purse and find great treasures: keys, a wallet, sunglasses.

We read books.

We dance to old rock 'n' roll songs.

And every single week, I can't wait for our time together.
I leapfrog from one Thursday to the next.

But this Thursday will not be happy. This Thursday, I can't be with you.

A nasty bug has gotten in our way.

Making people sick in one town after another.

You can't see it anywhere, but it's *everywhere.*

The bug jumps: from grandmothers to grandfathers, from moms to dads, from parents to kids. It makes them feel too hot, too achy, and too tired.

And, right now, nobody knows how to stop it.

The only way to be safe is to never leave home, so the bug can't find you.
That's why we can't be together.

So I'll stay inside thinking of you and the happy times we've had....

Playing horse and buggy as I pull you on your sled.

Splashing in rain puddles.

Listening to crows *caw* in the treetops at the park.

I'll watch old videos of you that make me laugh.

I'll FaceTime you, so at least we can see and hear each other.
We'll talk, but it won't be the same.
You stare at the magic screen, confused and wondering....
"Why don't you hug me and play with me?"

Then you look behind the phone to see if I'm there,
as if we're playing a game of hide and seek.

But no. I'm not there. I'm here.
Sitting in my house, missing you, as you sit in your house, missing me.

Maybe you even wonder if I still love you.

Harper! It's nothing like that!
I wait and wait, counting the days....

For that meanie bug to go away...

So once again we can have our Happy Harper Thursdays.

Fern Schumer Chapman (a.k.a. "Mama Fern") is a grandmother of one and an award-winning author of several books, including *Motherland* and *Is it Night or Day?*.

For more information about her work, please visit
http://fernschumerchapman.com

Phoebe Chandler Turner is a grandmother of two and a designer/illustrator.

The two friends and neighbors collaborated on this book while respecting social distancing during the 2020 Coronavirus shelter-in-place restrictions.